The Art Of Marriage Communication

Communication Habits That Will Kill Your Relationship And How To Do It Better

By

Nicolas Kelton

Table of Contents

Introduction

When relationships break down, it is mostly because of poor communication. Some people find it difficult to communicate because they're afraid of making themselves vulnerable, or they simply don't know how. Others have no problem expressing themselves, but their message gets lost in translation - often distorted by how the receiver interprets their meaning. A lot of times, the problem lies in poor listening skills.

This book addresses the various causes of unhealthy communication in relationships. It unravels both the simple and complex issues that arise from and cause poor communication between couples. It provides insights and solutions to help partners learn how to communicate openly and effectively and how to nurture healthy communication long-term.

This author has counseled hundreds of couples with communication problems and helped save numerous relationships-in-trouble through online and/or private sessions, as well as his self-help ebooks and programs specifically designed to resolve issues in communication.

How can this book offer a genuinely positive impact on your relationship? With the support of real and relevant studies, books, and concepts by reputable experts in the fields of psychology and couples' counseling/therapy, this author expands upon his own theories about how healthy communication can be cultivated and maintained to support happy, long-term relationships. This book also provides actual statistics where needed, as well as science-based evidence to further reinforce the author's approach to the subject matter.

By the end of this book, you and your partner will have a better appreciation for each other, despite your differences and the conflicts you've been struggling with. You will feel more comfortable opening up to each other, and you will find the motivation and the will to put in the work needed in order to improve the communication aspect of your relationship. Last, but not least, both of you will find a new and more effective and honest voice, so to speak, to help you express yourselves more capably, comfortably, and sincerely.

Sweeping your communication problems under a rug will only lead to unresolved issues piling up until your relationship falls apart under their combined weight. Addressing poor communication in your relationship can be uncomfortable, to say the least; it can be overwhelming and intimidating; at worst, it can cause all your pent-up negative thoughts and emotions to go off like a bomb. But with the help of this book, you and your partner can take small and easy steps towards communicating more openly and with kindness and respect.

Waiting until you or your partner feels comfortable enough to address the elephant in the room is not an option. A breakdown in communication has the tendency to cascade like an avalanche, destroying everything in its path. If you genuinely believe that your relationship is worth preserving, then you and your partner need to work hard to make it work by dealing with and finding a solution to your communication problems.

So turn to the next page, and keep the pages turning. Read every chapter and take every word to heart. Finishing this book is a critical first step towards a guaranteed lifetime of happiness and security with your partner.

Chapter 1 Love Is A Choice

It is often said that we do not choose who we fall in love with. It just happens, most of the time, unexpectedly. There's no rhyme or reason, initially. When it happens, you just know. The butterflies flutter in your stomach. You can't stop thinking about the person, so much so that you can't sleep. You can't erase the silly smile on your face when you receive a text message from them. You feel like you're walking on air. This is romantic love. It's idealized love. And there are countless people out there who experience it at least once in their life.

There is also a love that grows over time. It's like a planted seed, watered and nurtured into full bloom. It can take weeks, months, or years. Some are not aware it's even happening until the love has fully blossomed; others are aware from the get-go. But there is still a sense of falling - falling into the person; falling in love; diving into the scary but exciting experience with both feet.

Whether we realize it or not, our preferences actually determine, to some degree, who we fall in love with - be it spontaneous or gradual. During the initial attraction, we unconsciously or consciously make the choice to push through and explore the possibility of a relationship.

As we get to know the other person better, the love grows deeper. And each day, week, month, and year that passes, we make the choice to stay and keep making the relationship work. We choose the person we want to spend our life with, to keep loving, to take care of, to make happy.

The intense feelings we experience at the beginning of the relationship usually fades. As we slowly become more familiar with our partner and as we finally discover our joint rhythm, the love transforms into a calmer and more comfortable kind. And you will have to choose to do the work to stay in love and keep your love alive.

We know that love is not always going to be a bed of roses. We know that loving our partner means making a commitment to an imperfect person. Sooner or later, when the exhilaration of new love has passed, and our rose-colored glasses come off, the real work begins.

Because real and lasting love takes a lot of work - something the work is easy; other times it's emotionally, mentally, and physically exhausting. Every minute of every day that you stay in the relationship, you make the choice to do the work to keep the love going. In this sense, love becomes more than a feeling; it is a constant choice to stay committed to our partner despite the obstacles we encounter along the way.

Love becomes a choice every time we choose to forgive our partner for their shortcomings and mistakes; every time we choose to simply shrug our shoulders over their irritating quirks; every time we choose to look beyond their flaws and focus on the good; when we choose to support their dreams and comfort them through their disappointments and heartaches; when we choose to take care of them when it's easy and even when it's hard; and through every disagreement or fight and we choose to keep working to make the relationship work.

And there will be times when we'll feel unhappy in the relationship, and when choosing to keep doing the work will become more challenging. We might feel like we're the only ones pulling most of the weight, and it'll be too easy to forget why we keep choosing to love our partner. Because we do have a choice to stop, to walk away.

But when we choose to stay, we choose love once again. We choose to remember why we chose our partner to go through life with - through the good times and the bad, for better or worse. We choose to remember the reasons why we love them.

Real and lasting love is about making both the tough and easy choices that will benefit the relationship. It's about committing to these choices despite knowing that it will mean doing hard work at times. We choose to put in the effort because we know it's worth the rewards.

Genuine love is a deliberate choice - you plan to stay with and love your partner no matter what. You don't intend to abandon ship when the going gets tough. You brace yourself for the storms that may come and you weather them together.

Staying in love, nurturing your relationship, growing together and as separate individuals, and working towards a shared future requires effort; but most importantly, it requires both of you to make love your choice.

Choosing Love Is A Choice

Scenario 1

A man and a woman start dating. They get along well and both think that there is potential for a serious relationship in their near future. And then fate plays a cruel joke on them and strands them on an island. Having only each other for company, they are both appreciative of the fact that they have good chemistry, and that their strong physical attraction to each other actually gives their situation a romantic element. They feel lucky that, instead of being stranded on an island with somebody they didn't like or a complete stranger, they end up together.

They have already made an emotional connection, and have just begun to discover how much their minds also clicked. The challenge of surviving their unfortunate situation with nothing but their instincts and combined wits and skills seems less scary because there's already a sense of comfort and security between them; although still raw and abstract, it gives them something to hold onto - some hope in an otherwise hopeless condition.

Being thrown together to face such a daunting test reinforces their bond; they grow stronger as individuals, and also as partners. Their unique situation teaches them to accept each other's flaws; how to compromise for their mutual benefit; and the importance of the willingness to change for each other and for the betterment of their relationship. After all, all they have is each other. It is inevitable that what began as simple physical attraction, blossoms into love.

Their situation forces them to be dependent on each other, to work together, and to trust each other. As a result, they connect more deeply emotionally and their minds adapt in such a way as to complement each other. Even more importantly, they give each other sustenance - physically, emotionally, and intellectually; and they learn how to live in harmony despite their differences.

The elements put them to the test, both as individuals and as partners. And they pass with flying colors. Their individual natures also put their individual survival and that of their relationship at risk. But, together, they fight against the threats. One night, under the vast blanket of stars, they wonder what would have happened to their budding relationship if they weren't so unceremoniously removed from their civilized world and into the harsher conditions of the natural world.

They ask each other if the same, deep love and connection they now share would still have developed and if they would have still made the right choices for the sake of their relationship had they had been given a different set of challenges in their old life.

Scenario 2

The same two people meet under the same

circumstances and feel the same initial physical attraction. Fate decides to let their lives run their natural course. They go on normal dates and decide to commit to a normal, committed relationship.

Amidst their normal, individual lives, they find time for each other. Over time, the physical attraction only grows stronger and their emotional connection, deeper. They enjoy discovering their similarities, their common interests, their shared hopes and dreams. Their minds also find common ground.

Just like most couples on their honeymoon phase, they choose to see the great things about each other and to shrug off the flaws and quirks they didn't like about the other. There are a lot of things they didn't see eye to eye on; but, more often than not, they eagerly let these things go to avoid arguments. Enjoying each other's company is their priority.

Eventually, their individual lives bring conflict into

their relationship. His friends roast him for giving up the pleasures of the single life. Her career takes a lot of her time. Attention from other women distracts him and makes him wonder if he does want to be in a serious and committed relationship. She begins to wonder the same about him. He starts to get annoyed by what he considers her excessive neediness. She starts to feel neglected.

They could have talked about their concerns, but they're always too busy with "more important" stuff or they simply didn't want to have "those" conversations.

They are right for each other in many ways; they can be good for each other. But they fail to realize this and to appreciate the potential for the great life that they can have together. Their different perspectives are influenced by their individual circumstances, but they could have found a way to meet halfway and resolve their differences if they put in the time and effort.

Their differences soon make them forget that they used to share the same desire and hope to make their relationship work, and the reasons why they saw The One in each other. They have different priorities they could have worked out if they chose to. But they choose to allow these differences to become bigger than their love, and they unintentionally also choose to let these differences put a wedge between them. It becomes inevitable that their relationship soon falls apart.

Making Choices For Better Or Worse

Romantic relationships always involve making choices from the get-go. When it comes to choosing a long-term/lifetime partner, some prefer making informed choices; others choose to take a leap of faith. In both cases, once we choose to make a long-term/lifetime commitment to another person, all the other choices we make from thereon should support this first choice and, therefore, should be made mindfully and with a focused purpose.

A relationship is a partnership, with two people making coordinated efforts, day in and day out, to make their relationship work, to keep their love alive. These coordinated efforts include making carefully considered choices, whether individually or together. We have to remember that every choice we make on our own will affect our partner and our relationship; the same applies to our partner. Sometimes, we will not agree with the other person's decisions, and these are the instances that will test the strength of our bond with our loved one.

These are also instances when effective communication is crucial. Talking about our motivations and intent - the reasons behind our decisions - involves our partner in the decision-making process and lets them know that we value their input. It also shows that we understand how our choices should not only be about one person - that they will impact the other person as an individual, and both of us as a couple. Arguments may arise from our incompatible decisions, but these arguments can be constructive if we also choose to make them so.

Our choices can either benefit our relationship or hurt it. One choice always to lead another, which leads to another. There's always an opportunity to make things better, but our subsequent choices can also make things worse. A choice can lead to a power shift in the relationship; it can cause friction and animosity. It can also be a source of satisfaction and strength, especially if we make a choice with our partner.

Relationships often require the careful art of compromise, and when our choices are not in harmony with each other, we must learn how and be willing to meet each other part of the way. This could mean one person giving way to the other, making certain concessions, and giving our partner our patience and understanding when necessary. The flip side of this is that we can also expect to get the same from our partner when it's their turn to give us the same.

There are also times when we make choices without knowing what the outcome will be. When the outcome is negative and ends up causing damage and hurt, the intent usually becomes less important than the result. That is to say, it won't matter much if we did not intend to cause hurt; what will matter more is that we caused it and how we'll choose to fix the damage. And once again, the decision on how to proceed - how to resolve the problem - should be made together, in harmony.

When we take responsibility for our choices, we also take responsibility for the direction our relationship takes. Only when we realize this can we begin to make our choices work for us, instead of against us.

How our relationship evolves, and how we grow together as partners and as different people depend on each and every choice we make. Should we make the next move and schedule the next date? Should you accept the apartment keys he's offering and move in together? Is it time to introduce her to your parents? Do you say "Yes"? Should you accept that better job offer in another city? How do you tell him that you don't like his new female friend? How will you surprise her on your anniversary? What mistakes are you willing to forgive? Should you get angry because he forgot to call you when he said he would?

Committing to another person means making choices not just for ourselves, but also for the other person. This is not to say that the decisions we make will be unilateral; this means that every choice we make should also involve our partner - their thoughts and feelings on the matter, and the impact it will have on them.

Choosing where to eat; what movie to watch; where to live; our career path; our brand of toothpaste; what TV size to buy; how to discipline our kids - choices big and small will take two minds to make in order to maintain harmony in the relationship. Sometimes, serious conversations will be needed in order to resolve the situation. Other times, we will just know what the right choice is because we already have a good understanding of what we need from each other.

In the aforementioned, fictional scenarios, the different circumstances the couple were in seemed to "limit" their choices and, therefore, were pivotal to how their relationships turned out. While it is true, to some extent, that our circumstances determine what choices we have, it is just as true that the choices we make can also determine our circumstances. In both scenarios, how much the couple valued their relationship should be the pivotal factor.

Their circumstances tested their commitment to each other and, while these influenced their decisions with regards to their relationship, it was still their choice how they would let their circumstances influence their behaviors and mindsets. The scenarios may seem like an oversimplification of why relationships succeed or fail, but they serve to demonstrate that we should not let our circumstances distract us from prioritizing the things and people we value. Regardless of what life throws at us, we should always strive to make the right decisions for the people we care about and love.

When couples who have stayed married until their golden years were asked what their secret was to a lasting relationship, the common answer is this: every day, they chose each other. Every day, they chose to love.

Chapter 2 Why Working On YOU Is More Important Than Fixing Your Partner

Being in a relationship means growing together as a couple; but this does not preclude, nor does this prohibit, your continued growth as an individual. There is the romantic notion that being with the right person will make you feel whole; like a missing piece in a puzzle, the right person will complete the picture that is your life. And then two people become one.

This is true, to a certain degree. Your partner can provide you with the balance that you've always needed. A loving relationship can enrich your life in ways that make you feel more alive than you ever had before. At the same time, you tend to focus most of your energy, attention, and love on your partner. After all, you also want to be the one to give your partner the balance they've always needed; you also want to enrich their lives in ways that make them feel more alive than they ever had before.

This kind of give-and-take is healthy for any relationship. But it can also go wrong when you start to neglect your own needs and blame your partner for the feelings of neglect. The fact is, when you make your partner "your entire world" and forget yourself, that balance and enrichment you initially experienced can easily tip towards imbalance and diminishment, mostly within yourself.

When your needs become demands is when you'll start to feel that you're the only one who's doing all the giving. Whether or not your partner is doing their best to give back as much as you have, their efforts will fall short. And then you're feeling of being one with him will also start to crumble and be replaced by a feeling of un-togetherness.

And then the focus of your energy shifts towards finding fault in your partner and trying to fix them. What you fail to realize is that because you're the one who's been neglecting your needs, you're also the only one who can truly satisfy them.

In any relationship and in life, as a whole, you should be responsible for your own happiness and growth. You should feel complete, all on your own. You should work on yourself, for yourself. You owe yourself the kind of love and appreciation you're looking for. And you cannot expect somebody else to make all of these happen for you if you can't make them happen for yourself first.

Make Yourself Happy

Happiness is a choice; it's a self-fulfilling prophecy. Choosing to be happy is easier said than done, at least at first. But when you shift your mindset from expecting other people and circumstances to make you happy, to one that owns responsibility for making yourself happy, then you can begin to address and satisfy your own needs, and you can choose to celebrate you and your life in all sorts of ways.

Think about it this way: when you entertain negative thoughts, the thoughts get you down; they make you feel sad and, perhaps, even hopeless. So the opposite is just as true: when you choose to entertain positive thoughts, then your spirit will be uplifted; you will feel happy. You make happiness your choice.

You know what makes you happy, so do what makes you happy. It's normal to expect your partner to do these things for you, but it doesn't mean that you should stop doing them for yourself. Likewise, while you're making your partner happy, it should not come at the price of your own happiness.

And when you have personal happiness, you will also become more loving. When you choose to be happy, happiness also flows into your relationship.

Forgive Yourself For Your Mistakes And Shortcomings

But first, you should own them. And then you can learn from them, and this is when you grow. Remind yourself that your failings do not define who you are; choosing to learn from these failings and how you use them to improve your life are what will define you. Self-forgiveness is an important aspect of self-love. You have to learn to accept yourself for everything that you are before you can expect your partner to do the same for you.

When you lose yourself in your relationship, however, and when your top priority is no longer yourself, your mistakes and shortcomings may make you feel insecure. You may end up overcompensating, by neglecting your needs even more than you've already been doing and investing all your energy on your partner.

You are being dishonest with yourself when you avoid

acknowledging and forgiving your failings. Part of you will always be pretending that things are okay, while deep inside, feelings of dislike for yourself grow. And instead of learning from your failings so you can grow, the opposite happens - they make you feel less significant and trapped by your perceived limitations.

Your attempts to overcompensate may soon shift into finding faults in your partner and trying to fix those faults. But what you're really doing is avoiding fixing yourself. Should you be lucky enough to have an understanding and patient partner, one who adores you, mistakes and all, then their love and support can be an effective motivation for you to also embrace the person that you are, mistakes and all. Should you be unlucky enough to have a partner who judges you based on your shortcomings and makes you feel bad because of them, then it becomes even more important for you to forgive and love yourself in spite of them and use the lessons they offer to help you grow.

Remember that choosing to be happy also means learning to forgive yourself.

Change Yourself For The Better, For You

Some people mistakenly believe that finding and being with the right person is what will make their life better, that "The One" will make them want to "become a better person." So they wait, and they wait. And they fail to realize that the power to change their life and themselves for the better is in their hands, and the first step they have to take is a simple change in perspective.

We cannot change others; people only change when they're ready. This is why attempting to "fix" your partner - to make them change - is futile. And the same applies to you. Nobody but you can affect genuine change to your behavior, attitude, way of thinking, and way of life. You may be influenced by somebody else - a friend or loved one - to appreciate a different kind of food or enjoy a new activity, but the reason you were effectively influenced is that you genuinely loved it. They did not "make you" like something; they only helped you discover it. Similarly, nobody can make you like a movie, an author, or mountain-climbing if it just doesn't suit who you are.

The same principle applies to how and when you choose to change for the better. You decide how; you decide when. And, most importantly, you decide for whom you're doing it. And you should do it for yourself, because only then can you be sure that you're ready and willing to make the change. After all, the only behaviors and thoughts you can truly control - and, therefore, change - are your own

Working on you means loving yourself. It's something you owe to yourself. And doing so might even motivate your partner to do the same. They will definitely see you in a different light - a better light. You'll gain their admiration and respect all over again.

Working on you doesn't have to mean neglecting your partner. All these forms of self-love - choosing to be happy, forgiving yourself, and changing for the better - are, at least, just as important as making your partner happy, forgiving them, and helping them change for the better. Working on you creates a positive atmosphere that can cascade into all aspects of your relationship - the emotional, intellectual, and physical connections you share with your partner.

Chapter 3 Creating Intimacy

Intimacy, in all its forms, is integral to any successful relationship. Just as important as physical intimacy are our emotional and intellectual connections with our partner, and cultivating these connections requires satisfying our partner's needs for acknowledgment, appreciation, and acceptance.

Each of us has a definition of what an "ideal" partner is. We create standards against which we measure potential mates. More often than not, however, physical attraction comes first; getting to know the other person and finding out whether or not they meet our standards follow soon after. If you're extremely lucky, your partner would be exactly as you imagined them to be - exactly as the idealized version you've always dreamt of.

More often than not, too, we fall in love with a person even when they do not meet our "ideal partner" standards. Down the road, this can become a problem when we start to see more and more how they're "not perfect," and then these supposed "imperfections" can make us overlook and become unappreciative of what makes them good for us - the traits that made us fall in love with them in the beginning.

As we get to know our partner better, we can easily make the mistake of thinking that they're not the same person we fell in love with - that they have changed - when we finally discover parts of them that do not fit into the ideal picture we had created. So we start to compare them with how we visualized our ideal partner is supposed to be, and we try to change them to make them fit that idealized role.

The truth is, the right person for us does not necessarily have to perfectly meet our idealized standards. And while it can happen for some people, it doesn't mean that it's the only kind of real love. After the initial fall, we can learn to love our partner even more or in a new way when we choose to acknowledge, accept, and appreciate who they were when we first met, the real version of them that we're getting to know more deeply, and the person they will grow into in the future.

We can create greater and lasting intimacy, at every level, when we learn to embrace the whole package. Acknowledgment, acceptance, and appreciation of our partner will not only satisfy their needs but also our need to realize that they do not have to fit an ideal image to be ideal for us.

Acknowledgment

Genuinely acknowledging our partner is one of the most powerful tools we have at our disposal to nurture intimacy in our relationship. Proper acknowledgment means recognizing and affirming our partner's value - their presence and influence - in our life and as an individual.

When we acknowledge our partner, we:

- Encourage them to feel happy about themselves
- Lift their spirits and raise their self-esteem
- Create opportunities for meaningful conversations
- Gain a new perspective on our partner's worth and role in our life
- Inspire them to persevere and to love themselves
- Let them know that we understand what they're going through and they can depend on us

Feelings of neglect and loneliness often arise from lack of acknowledgment; and when the source of such negative feelings is someone we love, the hurt can turn into resentment. When this happens, we begin to push our loved one away or build a wall around ourselves to protect us from further pain. Intimacy makes us vulnerable, so we turn away from it.

Awareness of these consequences can help us be more sensitive to our partner's needs to be acknowledged. Making them feel good about themselves should make us feel good, as well, but more than that, acknowledging their value is an act of love that we should practice as often as possible simply because our partner deserves nothing less from us.

Appreciation

Appreciation is giving our partner positive attention which, in turn, creates positive feelings. And positive feelings - whether they're for each other, toward oneself, or for the relationship - fuel intimacy and keep a relationship going.

Appreciation and intimacy go hand in hand - one will fade without the other. This is why a lack of appreciation is one of the most common reasons that many relationships fail. Giving our partner constant appreciation, even for the most mundane things, might seem tedious; but it's a habit we'll have to cultivate and make the norm, not the exception.

We can show our appreciation through simple thank yous, compliments, and grateful gestures, such as an appreciative hug, a grateful smile, some thank-you pampering and gifts, and sincere efforts to make life easier and happier. Giving them our time and attention is, perhaps, the most profound way that we can let our partner know how much we appreciate them - what they have to say, the things they do, and their presence in our life.

Appreciating our partner should always be our priority. Appreciation is like water to a plant - it makes a person blossom. When we feel valued by those we also value the most - a desire that is common to everyone - we become more open to deeper levels of intimacy, which is an essential ingredient in any lasting relationship.

Acceptance

The longer we are in a relationship, the more behaviors

and characteristics we find annoying in our partner. This is mostly because our tolerance levels often get sorely tested by time. But by refocusing our outlook and shifting gears from annoyance to acceptance, we can remedy this particular and all-too-common hindrance to intimacy in long-term relationships.

Unconditional love, the purest form of acceptance, is easy enough to commit to at the beginning of a relationship. But, as the saying goes, "familiarity breeds contempt," and this usually happens to couples after being together for many years. It is important to remember, however, that this is not a foregone conclusion, nor is it a self-fulfilling prophecy. When we begin to understand that the bigger picture - our relationship - is more important than certain annoying details, then we can also begin to wholeheartedly accept our partner, warts and all.

It can be difficult to do at first, simply shrugging our shoulders when our partner leaves an empty milk carton in the fridge for the nth time, or when they do not clean up exactly the way we like it after they make a mess in the kitchen. But when we shift our perspective - when we look at the life we share with them in its entirety, we'll see that accepting our partner's flaws and loving them just the way they are count for so much more than wasting our energy on things we cannot change.

Because that is part of the fine print in any lasting relationship: There are things about our partner that we won't be able to change; these are part of who they are, and loving them means accepting the whole package. Accepting this truth is the first step toward real, unconditional love. With the acceptance of everything that is familiar about our loved one, there won't be any breakdown of the intimacy we share.

Creating and nurturing intimacy means allowing ourselves to be vulnerable. As Dr. Sue Johnson explains in her book, Hold Me Tight [1], being vulnerable also allows us to create a level of emotional safety with our partner which, in turn, helps strengthen our bond. We must remember that being vulnerable, just like all other aspects in a relationship, is a two-way street. Our partner needs to feel safe enough to reveal their true selves to us with the hope that we'll acknowledge, accept, and appreciate them for who they are. And we can make them feel safe by also revealing our true selves to them.

Chapter 4 Avoiding Fights

Fights are inevitable in a relationship; at the same time and to some degree, they're also healthy when we can be mature about solving the conflict and when we genuinely want to smooth things out. But we can and should avoid fights when they only serve to hurt the person we love and weaken the bonds that hold our relationship together.

Being Right Vs Being Loved

Fights between couples often turn into a power struggle - only one can come out on top. Neither we or our partner wants to be wrong. Fights can get ugly pretty quickly when it takes a you're-wrong-i'm-right turn.

When this happens, we need to take a step back until we have more control over our emotions, and especially until our love for our partner and their love for us become more important than our desire to be right.

Love is often placed on the backburner when pride takes over and being right becomes the main focus of a fight. While in the middle of it, we don't realize that winning could mean a big loss for the relationship because we end up hurting the person we love - with our words and especially with our misplaced priorities. In the end, nobody wins.

We have to ask ourselves, "Is winning an argument worth the cost of hurting our partner? Is it worth the cost of causing damage to our relationship?" What price are we willing to pay to be right?

But what if our partner is unequivocally wrong? Then there's no need to underscore the fact. Forgiveness is the only logical step to take if we want to resolve the conflict.

'How Might I Have Contributed To The Situation We Have Here?'

Saying Something Out Of Anger Or Hurt

We are at our most vulnerable when our emotions are running high - whether we're feeling extremely angry, frustrated, or hurt. When the need to express our intense feelings into words becomes overwhelming, we usually end up saying things we would later regret.

What we say during these moments and while in the midst of a fight may not accurately describe the reality of the situation, but it does rawly reflect the weight of our emotions as a result of past unresolved issues, present feelings of frustration and hopelessness, or future expectations of more problems and disappointments.

So whether or not the words we say in the heat of the moment may not be accurate, they're not completely irrelevant, either. They're valid to some extent - in terms of describing your emotional turmoil and especially in terms of the damage they can cause to the relationship.

Not saying how we feel - keeping our emotions bottled, especially for too long - is unhealthy, of course. This is another reason that cultivating healthy communications with our partner is extremely important. Whether or not we are able to do this, when we're in the middle of a fight and we feel our emotions about to explode into angry and painful words, putting a lid on our emotions is not always the best course of action. The pressure will continue building and you will still end up exploding.

The solution is to let the pressure out slowly. This is easier said than done; taking control over your highly volatile feelings is often a nearly impossible battle of mind over emotions. You will have to give expression to your emotions without flying off the handle. You will have to acknowledge your feelings, instead of denying them.

This requires preparedness and lots of practice. In anticipation of a fight - because you know that it'll happen sooner or later - start figuring out how you can modify your responses to the different possible triggers that you also know you'll encounter. Knowing how things can go wrong when you react a certain way, you can prepare in advance a different approach you can take without having to deny the intense feelings that will definitely arise.

At the start of a fight, whether it's expected or not, you should already prepare yourself for the possibility that your emotions will boil over. Take steps to release some of the pressure as early as possible. Take calming breaths. Close your eyes and think positive thoughts. Shift your focus. Take a quick walk outside. There are other ways to release the building pressure inside of you than blurting out angry and hurtful words.

Not Taking Responsibility For Our Feelings

In the book Crucial Conversations [2], co-author Joseph Grenny says, "The biggest unconscious mistake couples make is failing to take emotional responsibility for their feelings. We think others are 'making' us feel the way we are – and fail to see our role in our own emotions. That's why when we discuss our concerns with our loved one we are so often filled with blame and provoke defensiveness."

While our partner knows what buttons to push to trigger us, this does not justify nor take away our responsibility for how we react. When a fight becomes ugly because of how we react to something our partner says or does, we share half of the responsibility for it. Because no matter how hard we are pushed to our limits, we always have a choice on how to respond. And having a choice must also mean taking responsibility for that choice.

Not Listening To Our Partner

During a fight, we are usually on defensive mode and always ready with a response that we craft based on our own point of view of the issue. While our partner is taking their turn talking about their problem or side of the issue, we are more focused on what we are going to say next instead of focusing on what our partner is saying.

In the book After the Fight [3], the author stresses the importance of listening to our partner's perspective during or after a disagreement, as well as collaborating and restoring safety and goodwill.

When we fail to genuinely listen to our partner, we also fail to acknowledge their own point of view and how they feel. The message we send is that we do not believe their thoughts and feelings are valid.

Psychologist Faye Doell, in her 2003 study [4], said that people either listen to understand or listen to respond. And the only way to properly resolve conflict is when we learn to listen with the genuine purpose of understanding where our partner is coming from. Only then will we also be able to give them the response they actually need.

Listening to understand is a key ingredient in effective communication and, therefore, a healthy relationship. If we want to bring out positive changes in our relationship, we have to learn how to listen more deeply, and this will require simply hearing what our partner has to say, giving them our full attention, and doing our best to see things from their perspective. When they feel that they are being heard, they will tend to be more open and they will also be more willing to listen to us with the intent to understand and without judgment.

Not Being Emotionally Available

Not being emotionally available. Emotional unavailability, in itself, could be the main cause of most of our relationship problems. When we wall ourselves off every time a situation gets too emotionally intimate, we usually do it because we're afraid of being judged or hurt. Being emotionally unavailable, however, cripples our ability to communicate and makes communicating with us frustrating and even painful for our partner.

Successfully resolving any kind of conflict in a relationship requires us to be open about our feelings and to allow our partner emotional access. After all, being able to communicate with each other on an emotional level is essential to nurturing intimacy.

But before we can even remove a single brick from the wall we have built to protect our feelings, we should acknowledge our emotional unavailability and get to its root cause - our fear of being judged or getting hurt. One of the tests of a relationship's worth is our willingness to take that leap of faith - to trust that the person we love will catch us, accept us for who we are, and not hurt us. It's scary, but it's also liberating. We have to realize that our wall is not only keeping other people out; it's mostly keeping us in.

How To Never Argue Again/ How To Reduce Arguments

Joseph Grenny, also in the aforementioned book, shares that "[...] the biggest mistake that couples make is avoidance. We feel something but say nothing. At least until we can't stand it anymore. So we wait until we are certain to discuss it poorly before we bring it up. We tend to avoid these conversations because we are conscious of the risks of speaking up but unconscious of the risks of not speaking up. We tend to only weigh the immediate and obvious risks without considering the longer-term costs to intimacy, trust, and connection."

We must remember that bringing up a worry or an issue does not always have to turn into a fight. But when we postpone the discussion because it makes us or our partner uncomfortable, or because we think it will go away on its own, we actually increase the likelihood that the said worry or issue will lead to a fight sooner or later. Such unresolved concerns often do.

At the same time, as discussed in a previous chapter, there are certain aspects in our relationship and certain traits that our partner possesses that we simply have to learn to accept and, perhaps, even find endearing. Accepting things that we cannot change - things that do nothing more than cause us temporary annoyance or anxiety but do not really cause real and lasting harm - will make our relationship run more smoothly.

There are things that are just not worth a fight, things that we can just shrug off without them becoming seeds of growing resentment and unhappiness. We must consciously choose the things that really matter: spending a quiet night together, doing something we both love; sharing a typical breakfast on a typical weekend; or enjoying each other's company while doing chores or when on a long drive.

These are the small moments on which the foundation of a strong and steadfast relationship is built. When there are holes in the foundation, these small moments help fill them up. So, as much as possible, choose these moments over stuff that doesn't matter much in the bigger scheme of things.

How To Apologize Mindfully

When We Cause Unintentional Hurt

Here's the bottom line: at the end of the day, if we want to repair something broken in our relationship, we need to sincerely apologize to our partner regardless of whether or not we believe we are at fault. When we do or say something that offends or hurts our loved one, even if that wasn't our intention, we have to acknowledge their feelings, even if we do not feel that their reaction is justified.

(There is, of course, a limit to what we should apologize for - when doing so over and over only enables the other person and lets them get away with not taking responsibility for their own feelings.)

Oftentimes, our aversion to saying sorry is more about preserving our pride. But there are a lot of moments in our relationship when our pride creates a critical juncture between repairing a frayed connection and making the damage worse. We have to stop and examine not just our real intention, but also the unintended impact our words or actions caused.

Everything has consequences. The only difference is whether they are intended or unintended. When it comes to relationships, we have to learn to take responsibility and apologize even for the unintended ones when they cause our loved ones to get hurt. In such situations, the unintended impact should weigh more than our original intention because, after all, we still caused the hurt.

When our words or actions are interpreted in a negative way and different from what we intended them to mean, instead of being defensive, we should ask ourselves if there was a different way we could have done or said something. Instead of insisting that we did nothing wrong, we should simply apologize for the hurt we inadvertently caused.

Always look at the bigger picture. Our priority should always be to make things better. And if saying sorry is what is needed to do this, then we should not hesitate to say it and to mean it.

When We Make A Mistake

According to On Apology [5] author, Aaron Lazare, an effective apology can have any or all of the following parts:

1. *A valid acknowledgment of the offense that makes clear who the offender is and who is the one offended.* The offender must clearly and completely acknowledge the offense. This means owning responsibility for our mistake and sincerely apologizing for it.

2. *An effective explanation which shows an offense was neither intentional nor personal and is unlikely to recur.* Part of owning the mistake is giving our partner an explanation for our behavior, and especially making it clear that hurting them was not our intention. But it is important to remember that our explanation must not come out as an attempt to excuse or justify what we've done. It should simply clarify things for our partner, only if they need to know the hows and whys.

3. *Expressions of remorse, shame, and humility which show that the offender recognizes the suffering of the one offended.* Whether or not we

intended to hurt our loved one, and especially if we did, we should clearly express how badly we feel for the pain we have caused, and that we understand how we have hurt them. This is especially important when there is also a need to offer an explanation so that our partner does not feel that we are trying to excuse our actions.

4. *A reparation of some kind, in the form of real or symbolic compensation for the offender's transgression.* Part of a sincere apology is our willingness to learn from and pay for our mistake - to accept the consequences of our wrongdoing without complaint, be it in the form of less trust, lasting anger, lukewarm treatment, or diminished privileges, among others. The length of time for which we will have to "pay" may not be explicitly determined, but we should expect and be okay to wait until our partner has completely healed.

The promise of not making the same mistake again is,

of course, a given. Additionally, we should ask our partner what we can do - what they need us to do - to make things right. And most importantly, we should deliver on the promises we make. Changed behavior is the sincerest form of apology.

Lazare adds that "an effective apology must also satisfy at least one of seven psychological needs of the offended person."

1. *The restoration of dignity in the offended person.*
2. *The affirmation that both parties have shared values and agree that the harm committed was wrong.*
3. *Validation that the victim was not responsible for the offense.*
4. *The assurance that the offended party is safe from a repeat offense.*
5. *Reparative justice which occurs when the one offended sees the offending party suffer through some type of punishment.*

6. *Reparation, when the victim receives some form of compensation for his pain.*
7. *A dialogue that allows the offended parties to express their feelings toward the offenders and even grieve over their losses.*

Sincerity is critical to an apology. When we are able to say sorry from a place of remorse, shame, and humility, then all the pieces that will help us repair the damage we have caused will fall into their proper places in due time.

A mindful apology requires awareness of our role in the problem, how our behavior affected our partner, and how said behavior and how we choose to resolve the problem will impact the future of our relationship. It proves our acceptance of the repercussions of our actions and demonstrates our commitment to follow through on our promise to make things right and to change our behavior. It reasserts the fact that we appreciate having our partner in our life and that we are willing to do what's necessary to keep our relationship.

How To Create Lasting Harmony

Being in harmony with our partner means having the different parts of ourselves blending smoothly with each other. It is an effortless marriage of our ideas, feelings, and actions.

But creating lasting harmony takes a lot of effort, at least in the beginning. The effortlessness follows once harmony has been established. And when there's real harmony in the relationship, things continue to flow smoothly even when we encounter obstacles in our path.

Our ability to resolve conflict in our relationship and to get along despite our differences is pivotal in creating and maintaining harmony. More often than not, the conflict itself that causes discord in our relationship arises from the differences in our perspectives that have been shaped by a lifetime of personal beliefs, hopes, and experiences. The conflict serves as the platform on which these differences are put under a spotlight, and how we sort through these differences to find common ground determines whether or not we'll be able to resolve the issue and create harmony in our relationship.

Empathy and open-mindedness are essential tools in cultivating harmony, as these will help us become more accepting and understanding of each other's differences. We often end up getting hurt or hurting our partner when our differences get in the way, but we can avoid this by choosing to empathize with and keep an open mind about our partner's perspectives. We really have nothing to lose by doing so; we may even gain new and valuable insights. At the very least, having a better understanding of how and why our partner sees things the way they do will make it easier for us to accept certain things about them that we don't always agree with or approve of.

John Gottman in The Science of Trust [6] also emphasizes practicing empathy in order to stay connected despite our differences. He adds that being emotionally attuned with each other will help us respond appropriately to the other's bids for connection - this means simply opening our heart and mind to how our partner experiences and processes things so we can better understand their emotional responses to them.

We have to remember that while we are different from our partner in a lot of ways, our views have equal weight. Sometimes, we may have a better perspective; other times, our partner does. What is important is that we both learn to give way to each other, to be open to each other's input, to respect each other as equals, and to recognize that each of us brings value to the relationship. We only need to figure out how our different angles, curves, and patterns fit into each other; and if they don't, then we simply have to learn to make the necessary adjustments to accommodate the mismatch.

Chapter 5 How To Solve Problems

In her book, Blending Families [7], Elaine Fantle Shimberg says that poor communication is the main cause of all relationship problems. It naturally follows that working on effective communication is the key to solving problems, but it is a tricky feat that only the most committed couples succeed in doing.

Author and marriage and family therapist, Mitch Temple, elaborates on this in his book. He says relationships can succeed and overcome complex issues [8] when couples are willing to do the work necessary - whatever it takes - to tackle their problems and keep their relationship alive and kicking.

A breakdown in communication can quickly snowball into bigger and bigger arguments or an ever-widening chasm of unspoken hurt and resentment. This is why it's important to work together and figure out the best way to address our communication problems, first and foremost, as soon as possible, and in as many different ways as needed.

One such alternative to butting heads with our partner is what marriage expert Susan Heitler calls the "win-win waltz," in her book The Power of Two. This strategy involves tossing information back and forth until "we have an 'aha!' moment, and we come up with solutions that work very well for both of us."

Solving our relationship problems by addressing our communication problems will not only help minimize fights but also prevent the ugly feelings and physical side effects that often occur immediately after. We will not only repair and strengthen our bond with our partner but also ensure each other's overall well-being.

How To Get Your Partner To Really Hear You

Set The Date

Take some quiet time, alone, and figure out what

bothers you and why. Does it make you feel angry, worried, or hurt? Sort out your thoughts and feelings before attempting to have a talk with your partner.

Give your partner a proper heads-up that you want to talk. Let them know what you want to talk about, but make sure they understand that there's no need to feel threatened or defensive; there is no hostility or animosity. You just want the two of you to figure things out, together.

Set a time, much like you'd set a romantic date. Both of you will have to make the effort to fit this "date" into your schedule. If necessary, one or both of you might have to make some adjustments to accommodate the other's schedule. The time has to work for both of you as this will also influence the mood of your conversation. As much as possible, there should be no interruptions during those hours. You can do it in a public place, like a restaurant or a bar, or you can go someplace quiet and private. The important thing is that you both agree on the time and place and that both of you will be comfortable at the chosen location.

The day of your talk, and especially a few hours prior, make sure you're calm, clear-headed, and ready to listen, not just talk. Engaging in an activity that relaxes you will help.

The Talk

Begin with your usual pleasantries; ask about each other's day; talk about some of your minor plans. Both of you need to feel relaxed and comfortable in each other's company.

Take a deep breath, and let your partner know that you're ready to have the discussion. Start by describing to your partner how you see the problem - your perspective - and what your worries are. Make sure there's no anger or hint of an accusation; you're just describing how you specifically experienced the problem. Explain to them how it makes you feel and why. Ask your partner if he understands where you're coming from to make sure you're both on the same page. Ask them if there was anything you said that was unclear or that may have made them feel upset. And then take the time to calmly clarify the misunderstanding.

When you describe your point of view, always use "I" statements and avoid talking about your partner, as this might come across as you making presumptions and judgments. This will prevent your partner from feeling blamed and attacked. Again, just talk about yourself, your feelings, and your thoughts with no accusations or animosity.

While you're talking, be aware and sensitive to your partner's reactions. Acknowledge them; do not ignore them. If you see that your partner is getting upset, pause and ask them what you've said that caused them to get upset. And then give them the clarification and assurance they need. Do not get impatient or irritated; do not let negative thoughts and emotions get the better of you. Remember that you also do not want your partner to be overcome by hostility.

It's normal to also start feeling distressed when it seems that your partner is not being receptive to your efforts or they're not trying hard enough to understand your point of view. But keep your focus on the direction that you want this talk to take and your goal of clarifying things and resolving your communication problems. Switch gears when necessary; just keep your calm and focus.

Conversation Cues

- When you feel strong emotions starting to stir inside you or in your partner, alleviate the situation right away. Don't add fuel to the fire by responding negatively, with anger, irritation, or defensiveness.

- If emotions start to run high and your talk begins to take the form of a power struggle, it's okay to take a breather until both of you have calmed down again or to cease talks for the time being and try again some other day.

- As calmly as you can, make it clear that it's better to take a time-out, but you'd like to talk again. Don't just walk out without another word. Don't say you don't want to talk about it anymore.

- When you do get back to it and tempers start to get in the way again, repeat the process.

- If necessary, set up some rules; but both of you have to have input and the rules have to be acceptable to both parties.

- It's important that you both agree on the next step to take if you do need to take a time-out and reschedule.

- If you are able to say your piece without any emotional outbursts from one or both of you, ask your partner what they think and feel. And then it'll be your turn to listen.

- Remember to take turns talking, and take turns listening. Avoid contradictory words, as much as possible. As partners, you should be on the same page; if you're not, you should help each other get there.

- Use body language to let your partner know that you are listening. Don't get distracted by other stuff; don't let your attention stray.

- Both of you have to be genuinely open to what the other person has to say. You may not like some of it, and the same goes for your partner, but the goal of your talk is to sort through things to resolve the problem, not to prove that one is right and the other is wrong.

- If there is anything that is not clear, clarify before reacting.

How To Get Your Partner To Really Change

We can't get somebody to change unless they're ready and willing; and even then, it's best that they do it for themselves. But there are ways that we can influence our partner's behaviors - to inspire change. Needless to say, doing this is not about manipulation or selfish interests; it's to help resolve and move past relationship conflicts and preserve and strengthen the bond you share with your partner.

Get To The Heart Of The Matter

Immature. Insensitive. Selfish. We are all guilty of judging even those closest to us too quickly based on behaviors that we don't approve of. We are often guilty of not bothering to get to the heart of the matter - to understand the deeper motivations that cause them to behave in such ways. Before we can attempt to change any particular behavior, we must try to make sense of why they do it. This is different from finding an excuse for their flaws and bad behaviors.

The aim is to give them the benefit of the doubt and to learn more about what makes them tick, and why they refuse to or cannot seem to change. More often than not, unacceptable behaviors come from deeper issues that have been left unresolved for too long. This is where the aforementioned talk will be of great use.

Let Them Open Up

Actually verbalizing the root cause of their behavior must come from your partner; otherwise, it can come across as criticism or judgment, and you'll end up pushing them farther away and to be more resistant to change. Helping them acknowledge the deeper issues will make them more receptive to suggestions on how they can begin to change.

Sometimes, people do not know why they behave the way they do themselves because they have not taken the time to analyze their behavior and what's causing it. This will be a great opportunity for both of you to dig deeper and resolve buried issues. Just remind them constantly that you're there to listen without judgment.

Before doling out advice, restate the deeper issue to make sure you understand it clearly and to let them know that you listened and do understand. This will give them the assurance that you are not judging them and do not think less of them; your advice will carry more weight, and they will be more willing to hear your thoughts and motivate them to start the process of change.

Walk The Talk

Do as you say, and say as you do. You cannot expect your partner to do something you're not willing to do yourself, after all. And mimicking is an innate behavior, particularly when it involves a person we care for, admire, and respect. Use this to your advantage. This works in much the same way that partners learn to enjoy the other's interests. Telling them how they can do things differently can be effective when your heart-to-heart talk is successful, but showing them how is another compelling way to influence them.

Draw Reasonable Lines

There are behaviors that are like small drops in the water that only create insignificant ripples of irritation which eventually fade. These behaviors, you can learn to accept and maybe even find amusing and endearing farther down the line. And then there are problem behaviors that create a big splash that wildly rocks the boat you're both in and risks one or both of you getting hurt. These are behaviors that have the greatest potential to break your relationship - and you have to make your partner understand that the problem behavior is THAT serious.

When you have the talk, explain to your partner why you have to draw the line. Be as specific as possible as to how the problem behavior makes you feel - afraid, worried, angry, neglected. Help him understand how important it is for you and for the sake of the relationship that they change. You are not giving an ultimatum; it's a matter of figuring out the things that matter to both of you, as a couple and as individuals.

Reciprocate

You have to be willing to change, as well, to better yourself and your relationship. Remember that you and your partner are equals and that a healthy relationship is a give-and-take relationship.

How you feel about some of your partner's behaviors, they also feel about some of yours. When you make the effort to improve yourself, you will inspire your partner to do the same. And when you're both ready to do what needs to be done, you will not only become better as individuals but also as each other's partner.

The Magic Ratio

"[...] for every negative interaction [9] during conflict, a stable and happy marriage has five (or more) positive interactions." The 5 to 1 magic ratio was arrived at by Dr. Gottman and Robert Levenson after conducting a decade-long study of couples and how conflict resolution can predict whether or not the marriages were happy and stable. Their discovery helped them predict with over 90% accuracy which marriages would end up in divorce.

According to Dr. Gottman, negativity in any form wields such great emotional influence that it requires at least five positive interactions to cancel it out during a conflict. Healthy marriages, more often than not, are able to achieve this magic ratio; and, vice versa, the magic ratio helps ensure healthy relationships.

Knowing this, we can consciously and intentionally aim for this magic ratio whenever we have to tackle a problem in our relationship. Anger, which is the most common negative element during any conflict, counts as a single negative interaction. We can overcome it with positive interactions such as genuine interest in what our partner has to say, verbal or physical expressions of affection, simple acts that remind our partner that we care about them, intentional appreciation of the things that you love about our partner, empathy, heartfelt apologies, accepting the differences in our points of view, and humor.

It is important to remember that we should limit the

negative interaction to just one, as much as possible. Otherwise, having to compensate with more positive interactions will feel like too much work and can become too exhausting.

Repairing Trust

In the book, Eight Dates: Essential Conversations for a Lifetime of Love [10], the authors list steps to help fix broken trust: dedicating some time to talk about the problem; identifying and talking about our feelings without blame or criticism; listening to our partner without judgment; explaining things from our perspective; assessing how each of us contributed to the problem and taking responsibility for our roles; apologizing and accepting our partner's apology; and developing a plan so that the breach of trust won't happen again.

One or both of you will make mistakes that will make one question whether or not the other is trustworthy; some loss of trust may be acceptable and survivable.

But then there are acts that can completely shatter one's trust and make repairing the damage extremely difficult.

You not only lose the feeling of safety and security with your partner; to a considerable degree, you also lose emotional connection with them. We also feel vulnerable and doubtful towards ourselves; after all, how could we have let the betrayal happen?

Being betrayed by the person you love and trust is often the worst thing that can happen in a relationship. But if you and your partner are both willing to work on repairing the damage and saving the relationship, then repair it you must.

Do Not Blame Yourself

You can try to understand the situation without blaming yourself for the betrayal. We have no control over how other people choose to behave, especially when they choose to lie, be unfaithful, or secretive.

Everybody deserves complete honesty, loyalty, and faithfulness from their partner. Receiving anything less does not make you less of a person. Your partner's betrayal is a reflection of who they are, not who you are. To start the process of moving forward, accept the fact that there was nothing you could have done differently to prevent what happened. If you do believe that there are things you can change about yourself to help rebuild the trust, then do so but do not forget your worth, even with all your flaws.

Forgive

This is an absolute necessity to be able to truly move forward. You cannot have your partner's betrayal hanging over their head indefinitely. You cannot keep throwing it in their face whenever you feel upset and are arguing. You will have to find it in yourself to be at peace with what happened, to let it go, to let your anger go, and to forgive your partner.

The reluctance to let your partner off the hook often stems from pride or, to be more specific, hurt pride. It is a common coping mechanism when one has been betrayed. Forgiving your partner will require humility on your part - swallowing your wounded pride and allowing yourself to be humbled by the experience. Doing this will put you on equal footing with your partner - a place where nobody is better than the other, despite their mistakes.

And from this place, you will have a change in perspective and truly see that your partner deserves to be given the chance to regain your trust because they are still the same person you have always loved.

When you freely choose to forgive, you choose to free yourself from all the negative thoughts and emotions that were kindled by the betrayal. When you choose to forgive, you're not just doing it for your partner; you're also doing it for yourself.

Have Faith In Yourself

Another reason that some of us find it nearly impossible to move on after a betrayal is a nearly debilitating fear of being betrayed again and experiencing even worse pain and shame the next time around. Knowing firsthand how harrowing the experience can be, it's understandable that you wouldn't want to go through it again and to think you wouldn't be able to survive another betrayal.

But you have to have faith that you'll be okay, whether or not your efforts to save your relationship succeeds; whether or not your trust is betrayed once again. Obsessing over what might happen is as futile and unhealthy as obsessing about what already happened. You cannot change the past, and you cannot control how your partner will choose to behave after being given a chance to earn back your trust.

What you can control, however, is how you react to a situation. It's normal to anticipate the worst; it will help you prepare. But once you've figured out how you'll handle it, should it happen again, you can tuck it safely away in the back of your head, confident in the knowledge that you'll be alright. After you've done this, you'll also more confident about moving forward and wiping the slate clean.

Learn To Trust Again

Learning to trust again is a leap of faith. But at the same time, you have the means to assess the situation, and you can do so from an analytical perspective. While you cannot accurately predict your partner's future behavior, you have new information to factor into the equation and help you gauge whether their betrayal is an inherent character flaw or a random occurrence.

If you honestly believe that your partner deserves another chance, then give it. Wipe the slate clean. It's easier said than done; after all, you learned the hard way that there is no guarantee that the person you love will not hurt you again in the same way. There is no guarantee that they will value the trust they will have to work hard to regain and not break it again. There is no guarantee that they will always make the right choices for your relationship.

There are no guarantees, and you'll have to accept this fact and decide if you're ready to take the risk and give your relationship the chance to move forward in a healthy way, with no fear or anger. Only time will tell if your partner will be deserving of your trust. You can be prepared for another betrayal but only in the way that you already know how you'll handle it, should it happen again. After all, there are also no guarantees that the past will repeat itself.

So if you decide to learn to trust again, do so with a peaceful heart and an open mind. This is the only way to give your relationship a genuine chance to survive.

No relationship is perfect; even the most ideal ones go

through conflict once in a while. But you have control over how you'll react to whatever adverse situation that might arise. And you and your partner can take steps to prevent certain problems from becoming a threat to your relationship. This is why effective communication is key to avoiding, managing, and resolving issues. You and your partner have to be on the same page and to work together toward the same goal.

Chapter 6 Keeping Love Alive Long-Term

In psychology, there is a learning process called "habituation," defined as the decreased response to a repeated stimulus, i.e., when an individual is repeatedly exposed to a stimulus, he eventually learns to ignore it.

Habituation often develops in long-term relationships when a couple gets used to each other, so much so that the predictability of their daily life becomes boring - unstimulating. This happens when both parties simply stop trying; when they no longer work hard at keeping things interesting, and when they are no longer interested in making an effort.

The smile that used to bring you joy becomes all too familiar, so it soon gets ignored. And you also no longer make an effort to give your partner cause to smile. The kiss goodbye when leaving for work that used to give you comfort becomes part of the routine, so it soon gets ignored. And it doesn't become a big deal when your partner sometimes forgets; or, perhaps, they no longer feel the need to keep doing it.

Every relationship ultimately reaches a plateau. But you and your partner can easily prevent your love from completely flatlining or, worse, from descending into complete failure if you're both willing to do the work necessary to keep your love strong and alive. Your relationship may have lost the initial "magic" that made it romantic and exciting, but the next direction it takes is still within your control.

This means actually taking control of the wheel and actively enjoying each other's company and making sure the other is happy as you continue your journey together.

Arthur Aron, a research professor at Stony Brook University in New York and co-author of the study, "The Experimental Generation of Interpersonal

Closeness: A Procedure and Some Preliminary Findings," [11] which uses 36 questions to create intimacy in a lab setting, applied the same questionnaire in another study using a two-couples approach to determine "how self-disclosure can rekindle romance in long-term couples." [12]

They worked on the theory that, "when you're first in a romantic relationship, there's an intense excitement, but then you grow used to each other. If you do something new and challenging, that reminds you of how exciting it can be with your partner, it makes your relationship better." (Ibid.)

Below are strategies to keep your relationship going strong year after year, and even decade after decade.

The Importance Of Quality Time

Quality time does not have to mean extravagant vacations. You can have quality time with your mate when you prepare meals together, go shopping together, go for a run or a hike, learn a new skill, or just sit side by side while reading or watching your favorite movie or TV show. These activities may seem mundane, but these are the shared routines that also bring comfort and security to the relationship.

As ordinary as they may seem, these shared experiences become shared memories that accumulate and shape the story of your relationship. They also encourage and nurture intimacy.

Just as important as spending time together is how you spend it. According to another research by psychologist Arthur Aron, titled "Couples' Shared Participation in Novel and Arousing Activities and Experienced Relationship Quality," [13] reveals that love can be improved when couples explore new and challenging activities. Injecting adventure into your lives can benefit your relationship when you and your mate share the thrill, fear, and sense of accomplishment the experience brings.

Whether it's a physically challenging task such as bungee jumping, or a mentally stimulating activity such as trivia night, experiencing the intense emotions together will make you feel closer to each other. The added oomph to your normal routine will also keep the negative effects of monotony at bay.

Of course, going on regular romantic dates and anniversary getaways are a must. These serve as a constant reminder of your commitment to each other; they also serve to rekindle the passion that usually flickers in and out as the years go by if it doesn't get completely snuffed out.

The book, Eight Dates [14] authored primarily by John and Julie Gottman, can be a meaningful experiment that we can participate in with our beloved. As the title itself says, the book outlines eight, intentional, and conversation-based dates. It may sound unromantic, at first, going on dates that come with instructions, like each one is simply a task to be completed. But each date is designed to help couples strengthen their connection, rekindle intimacy, and discover new things about each other.

The eight dates focus on the following themes:

1. Trust & Commitment
2. Addressing Conflict
3. Sex & Intimacy
4. Work & Money
5. Family
6. Fun & Adventure
7. Growth & Spirituality
8. Dreams

The insights we discover on these Eight Dates can prompt difficult but meaningful conversations. They can also motivate us to go on more intentional dates with our partner; to invest the time and money to spend genuine quality time with each other because we'll realize that there will always be more to learn about each other.

Spending quality time with our mate offers both of us a chance to get comfortable enough with each other to open up about things that often go unsaid within the hustle and bustle of our daily lives. Or it can serve as an opportunity to simply reconnect, reminisce together, and make plans for the future.

The Importance Of Physical Touch

"Is Long-Term Love More Than A Rare Phenomenon? If So, What Are Its Correlates?" [15], a study from Stony Brook University, spearheaded by Daniel O'Leary and published by The Journal of Social Psychological and Personality Science, revealed that one of the key ingredients to having intense love in a long-term relationship is, unsurprisingly, physical affection and sex.

Physical affection and love often go hand in hand, and the results of the aforementioned survey add further proof to this. Simple physical demonstrations of affection, such as hugging and kissing, are major factors in sustaining intense love long-term. While a high frequency of sex was strongly associated with how intense long-term love was, the researchers also found that it was not always a requirement.

Conversely, surveyed couples whose relationships no longer involved physical demonstrations of affection also disclosed that love was no longer present.

In relationships where levels of physical affection were high, the intensity of love was also high even if there was some degree of dissatisfaction in the relationship. Physical demonstrations of affection clearly make up for whatever negative elements long-term couples normally have to deal with.

In the book, The Art of Seduction [16], author Robert

Greene explains the role of surprise in seduction and keeping the romance alive. When things become familiar and one or both parties in the relationship are no longer surprised by the other, the seduction also goes out the window, and physical intimacy soon deteriorates, as well.

There is no denying the extreme significance of physical touch in sustaining long-term love. The simple act of holding each other's hands while walking, kissing each other goodnight every night, rubbing against each other's arms while preparing food in the kitchen, or just placing your hand on the other person's back for no particular reason, through these physical demonstrations of affection, you're telling your partner, "I'm glad you're here. I want you here with me."

And then there is the obvious fact that being physically desired by your partner nourishes the intimacy in every level - physical, emotional, and intellectual.

Having a healthy sex life keeps things exciting; and the satisfaction both of you get from it feeds fuel to the fire, so to speak, so that your physical intimacy becomes self-sustaining.

The sex doesn't always have to be spontaneous. If necessary, make a schedule. This does not mean that you and your mate will simply be going through the motions. You can still make it exciting by planning for it and building up the anticipation, and making it fun or romantic, or both.

At the same time, you and your partner should actively participate in sustaining love. Both of you have to make the effort to remain desirable to the other, and to make each other feel desired. You have to put in the work and establish constant physical contact - in a variety of forms - as the norm, something that you do unbidden, something that becomes as natural as breathing.

But then the question of whether or not normalizing physical affection might lead to "habituation" also comes up. How can you prevent the stimulus - physical touch - from becoming unstimulating or, worse, boring?

The answer is, if the love is genuine, there is no risk that physical demonstrations of affection that become normalized will lose their touch, pun intended. It is one of those universal truths in lasting relationships, that the magic of touch never fades, even after the excitement of new love has. Everyday physical intimacy, no matter how simple, provides daily nourishment to your relationship.

It can be scientifically explained: oxytocin, the love hormone, is released when we are hugged by our mate and during orgasm. So, it can be safely said that normalized physical affection is an exception to the perils of habituation in long-term relationships. Physical contact is a powerful means of communication and is also the most intimate form.

The Importance Of Emotional Communication

Discussing his observations of how the participating couples in his study interacted with each other, in his book The Relationship Cure [17], Dr. John Gottman writes, "But after many months of watching these tapes with my students, it dawned on me. Maybe it's not the depth of intimacy in conversations that matters. Maybe it doesn't even matter whether couples agree or disagree. Maybe the important thing is how these people pay attention to each other, no matter what they're talking about or doing."

He concluded that the level of attentiveness that we give to our partner, whether during mundane moments or during fights, plays an important role in the success of a relationship. The results of this study led Gottman to one of his groundbreaking principles for successful relationships: making and accepting bids for connection.

Gottman defines a bid as "the fundamental unit of emotional communication." It can take any form, shape, or size; verbal, physical, big, small, a question, a statement, funny, serious, or sexual.

We make subtle bids all the time, mostly because putting ourselves out there - candidly expressing our desire to connect - is scary. So, we make bids for connection by asking questions, sharing stories, or with physical gestures, such as a simple touch on the arm. And then we wait to see if and how our partner will react - whether they'll accept our bid and respond accordingly, ignore our bid and turn away, or reject our bid and turn against it with an attack or argument.

In the aforementioned study by Gottman and his colleague Robert Levenson, they discovered that relationship masters made and accepted bids 86% of the time, whereas relationship disasters only did so

33% of the time. They further concluded that successful bids should be more about daily attention and less about grand gestures.

The level of the emotional connection we have with our partner can be measured by how we respond to each other's bids. If we are committed to keeping our relationship healthy, we should learn to pay closer attention to each other's bids for connection so that we can give the appropriate response. When we unintentionally miss these bids or intentionally reject them, we create and enlarge an emotional gap in the relationship. And, more often than not, this gap becomes filled with built-up resentment.

Making eye contact; responding to their sighs; touching them often; putting our phones down when they have something to share - giving them our attention as often as possible, and especially every time they need it - these responses strengthen our emotional connection with our partner.

The Importance Of Relationship Goals To Make Your Bond Stronger

Shared goals mean shared motivations and mutual understanding of each other's needs and desires. And when you work together with your partner to achieve these goals, the shared experiences - both good and bad - serve as ties that bring you closer to each other. Discuss the following goals with your partner; how you can overcome the obstacles that get thrown in your way; and what you need to do to achieve them.

- Making your relationship the number one priority every, single day.
- Enjoying each other's company, with no distractions, for at least half an hour every day.
- Always communicating with each other with kindness and respect.
- Making the other feel safe and secure when they allow themselves to be vulnerable.
- Working on creating more fun times together.

- Learning each other's non-verbal cues for affection and intimacy and responding appropriately.
- Going on regular dates and keeping the romance alive.
- Working on maintaining a healthy and satisfying sex life.
- Learning more about each other's sexual needs.
- Constantly making each other feel desired and cherished.
- Surprising each other with thoughtful gifts and gestures, whether or not there's a special occasion.
- Making plans for and going on trips as a couple
- Supporting each other's personal goals.
- Helping each other grow as individuals.
- Regularly engaging in a shared activity, such as a sport or a hobby.
- Learning something new together, such as salsa dancing, pottery, a new language, or first aid.
- Disconnecting from the world, especially the internet, and spending time in nature together.
- Giving each other some much-needed time alone to relax - such as a day at the spa, an overnight

staycation at a hotel, or just taking care of the kids the whole weekend.

- Having scheduled talks to discuss your relationship goals, where you are, and what you can do to keep moving forward.

Top 3 Science-Based Tips To Better Communicate With Your Partner

How many times have you heard the timeworn advice that "Good communication is key to a successful relationship?" Even marriage/couples counselors tout this as the golden rule. But, ironically, it is easier said than done.

Communication in relationships is sometimes like wading through murky and uncertain waters. Use the following science-backed ways to effectively communicate with your partner as a guide, and you might be surprised at the results!

Engage In And Appreciate Small Talk

In a paper written by John Gottman and Janice Driver [18], they revealed that "the mundane and often fleeting moments" in a couple's life can affect the health of their relationship in a greater capacity than serious and deep conversations can.

As you and your partner fall into a comfortable routine, the small conversations you have about seemingly insignificant details or happenings eventually become white noise. In one ear and out the other. One or both of you might even start to find these idle talks dull and tiresome. But these humdrum moments are still shared moments, and when taken together, they tell a beautiful story of intimate togetherness.

So, next time your partner tells you about his annoying co-worker or her movie date with girlfriends, take the time to appreciate the moment; show more interest, ask questions. Your partner will definitely be delighted and reciprocate the gesture.

Be Present In And Share The Mundane Experiences

An article in Psychology today mentions a Psychological Science study that discovered that talking about shared experiences improves a couple's closeness [19]. And this applies to experiences big and small.

This is a pretty straightforward way of rekindling your intimate connection with your partner if it has been lacking lately, or of reinforcing it.

The opposite is just as true: intentionally sharing even the most mundane experiences - being in the moment with your partner - can help improve communication in your relationship. Remember that communication is not restricted to words; non-verbal communication in the form of your behaviors and reactions towards your partner is just as meaningful. And the intimacy you create will definitely make way for deeper conversations.

Listen With Sincerity

As another oft-repeated saying goes, "Communication is a two-way street." A breakdown in communication between a couple does not only happen when communication is lacking; it also happens when one or both parties do not know how to properly listen to what the other one is saying.

When you listen carefully, you're also more likely to respond correctly. However, what often happens is that one or both of you respond emotionally, which is understandable when emotions are running high. During confrontations such as this, when your "communication" is going nowhere, it's important to take a breather, both literally and figuratively. Active listening can only occur when your mind is clear and your emotions are calm. A lot of misunderstandings between couples happen simply because they don't listen properly; a lot of these misunderstandings can be prevented by simply asking the other person to clarify.

During ordinary conversations, when it feels so easy to tune out your partner, don't. Give him/her your attention so that when you smile or nod in response, you don't do so absently. As with numbers 1 and 2, being engaged and in-the-moment makes a huge difference in effectively connecting with your partner.

Chapter 7 Exercises/Techniques For Communication Mastery

Allot one hour, every day or every weekend, to engage in an honest, non-judgmental, undemanding, heart-to-heart conversation. Make sure you won't be interrupted. Leave your phones in another room, or turn them off.

Play calming music or sounds. Sit with your back to each other, or facing each other and with your knees touching. You can hold hands. Or lie down on the bed or the floor, side by side, back to back, or facing each other. You can also dim the lights, and light some scented candles.

Make sure neither of you is feeling any intense emotion before you begin your session. Make the effort to calm yourself - your feelings and thoughts - before each session. This is critical to the purpose of this exercise, which is to facilitate effective communication between you and your partner.

It would help to have the following exercises printed on index cards so you and your partner can be guided better, at least until both of you have established your own routine and found your own flow. It is also okay to plan ahead as to what you intend to say during the coming session.

Express Appreciation

The longer you stay together as a couple, the easier it becomes to neglect the small things that you do for each other. Lack of appreciation can become the norm and consciously or subconsciously, feelings of sadness and resentment can grow.

Perhaps because saying "Thank you" is such a simple gesture, it's also a very simple thing to do away with it. While it's also true that couples with a deep enough connection do not need to say the words to let their partner know that they are appreciated, this verbal expression of gratitude, as mundane as it is within the bigger scheme of your daily lives, actually still carries a lot of weight and makes a huge difference, whether you realize it or not.

If you and your partner have been having communication problems, this practice of expressing appreciation is one of the most effective ways to make communication comfortable again. Proactively expressing gratitude also requires proactively taking notice of the good things, both big and small. As a result, you also end up having a better appreciation of what you have together. So you won't just be doing it to make your partner feel appreciated; you will also be reminding yourself of the reasons why you should feel grateful to have your partner in your life.

- Thank you for <doing/saying this> earlier.
- Thank you for taking the time to < ... >
- I am grateful knowing I can talk to you openly.
- I appreciate you and everything you do.

- I appreciate your < ... > (Mention a different attribute each time.)
- You make me feel happy when you < ... >
- I value your < ... >
- Our relationship is special to me because < ... > (Mention a different reason each time.)
- When you're not around, I miss < ... > (Mention something different each time.)
- I don't want to lose < ... > (Mention something different each time.)

Share Something New

It's too easy to make assumptions that are often far from the truth when one of both partners neglect sharing new information with each other. Even the smallest undisclosed tidbits can cause suspicions and encourage mistrust. The information might seem trivial to you and not worth sharing, but to your partner, and especially when not sharing becomes a habit, the mere act of not sharing is enough to trigger worry and suspicion; "Why didn't he tell me?" "If it's really nothing, then why did she hide it from me?"

Not sharing certain details that affect your mood and, therefore, other aspects of your day can also quickly cascade into misunderstanding and arguments. Your partner would not understand why you're short-tempered after a stressful day at work, and it would be unfair to lash out at them when you're upset about something else. Talking to them about your experiences, however, will not only help you get much-needed release but also will also prevent misunderstandings and make your feel partner more involved.

- I talked to < ... > today.
- I'm not looking forward to < ... > this morning/tomorrow/later this week at work.
- I ran into <...> at the supermarket earlier.
- I have this idea about starting <a new hobby/activity/sport>.
- I tried <a new food/drink> earlier and I loved it!

Friendly Inquiries

If you don't understand something, ask. We are often reminded of this growing up, especially in school. And this reminder is just as important in cultivating healthy communication in relationships.

There are times when it might be hard for our partner to open up because they are feeling overwhelmed by their feelings, or their thoughts are too muddled. You have gone through something similar yourself and you should use this experience to help you keep an open mind and to be more patient. Instead of making assumptions that can only worsen a potentially volatile situation, give your partner the benefit of the doubt, some time to calm down, and the chance to share with you why they were feeling down or angry the other night; why they've been absent-minded or distracted; why they've been stressed and ill-tempered.

Right timing is critical. Your friendly and concerned inquiry can come across as nagging or antagonistic if it is ill-timed, so patience and delicacy are also important.

When you're the one going through an episode of emotional or mental commotion, and you have enough clarity and calmness, as well as the need to talk about it, then do just that. Ask your partner for their insight; ask them to help you figure things out. Even if you do not find the answers you're looking for, communicating with your partner will help both of you get a better handle on the situation, and misunderstandings can be avoided.

- Why were you upset earlier?
- Anything interesting happened at work today?
- Did you have a tiring day?
- How did your meeting/presentation/interview go?

- I was talking to < ... > about < .... > earlier, and I don't know why I got upset. Maybe you can help me figure it out.

- What are you looking forward to today?

Reasonable, No-Blame, And No-Judgment Requests

Sooner or later, you'll find some of your partner's behaviors frustrating, even annoying. Perhaps these behaviors are recently acquired, or they've always been there but didn't bother you before.

Firstly, you have to realize that there are some characteristics and quirks that you may find less than endearing in your partner, to say the least, but which are not that significant when you consider the big picture. Things like a household item that you think is ugly but which has sentimental value to your partner, or painting the living room a color you don't particularly like, or a boisterous friend you find irritating but can tolerate in small doses - things like these, you can and should give a pass. Don't forget that you have your own stuff that your partner is willing to live with because they come with the package that is you.

But behaviors that actually cause some degree of hurt, worry, dissatisfaction, or unhappiness should be addressed. When you do, you should do so with care, and with no intention of making your partner feel bad about themselves. Your only intention should be preventing a future avalanche of built-up resentment. It is important that when you decide to bring up such an issue, your partner is aware of what is happening; they should know what to expect. They should not feel blindsided or attacked. This is where the relevance of establishing these communication exercises as part of your daily or weekly routine comes in.

Keep in mind that your requests should not be made into no-questions-asked demands or even ultimatums. Give your partner some latitude and room for error.

Missing a beat every now and then is normal and can be given a pass. Of course, some gentle nudging may also be in order to remind your partner that they're missing a beat.

- Please give me a call, or send me a message, if you'll be coming home late from work.
- It upsets me when you < ... >
- I'd appreciate it if you could help me with < ... > from time to time/every day.
- Would you mind doing the dishes/laundry every weekend?
- Perhaps we should make our bedroom a no-phone zone, what do you think?
- Please send me a quick message when you land or after you check into your hotel.
- I'd appreciate it if you could try not interrupting me when I'm speaking.
- I'd appreciate it if you would give my suggestions more consideration.
- I wish you'd show more interest in some of the things that interest me.

- It would mean a lot to me if you would support me in this particular endeavor.

- It would mean a lot to me if you could let me know what you think about < ... >

- I hope you'd understand why I draw away from you when < ... >

- When you < cite specific behavior >, it triggers < cite specific emotion > in me; please be more considerate. Perhaps we can figure out a way to better express ourselves when we find ourselves in a similar situation in the future.

- Please talk to me and let me know when I do or say something that triggers you, instead of just walking away.

Open Up About Hopes

Who else should you share your hopes and dreams with other than your partner? Doing so will remind both of you of the future you have yet to experience together; the memories you have yet to make. No matter how trivial, how big, or how soon or far into the future your hopes are, they can get your relationship back on track and keep you moving forward.

Talking about tomorrow, next week, next month, or the next few years is a great way to reconnect, and an even better way to let each other know that you still value each other's company and that you're looking forward to being together for many more years, despite the challenges you've faced. Even if your hopes only involve you, sharing them with your partner will assure them that they are still included in your life.

- A whole weekend disconnected from the internet could be immensely fun. We can go hiking or camping.
- I hope I/you won't have to work this weekend so we can have a movie date/go dancing.
- Maybe we should start planning that trip to Europe/the Caribbean we've been talking about for years.

- I hope we can finally have our second honeymoon on our coming 10th/25th anniversary!
- I'd love to finally be able to go on that month-long cruise with you.
- I hope I can have a spa day when this project is finally over.
- I'd love to start taking yoga classes soon.
- I hope I can go out with the guys/my girlfriends one of these nights.
- Anything special you're looking forward to tomorrow?
- What goals do you have for this month/year? How can I help?

Questions To Practice Active Listening And Nurture Deeper Intimacy

As mentioned in a previous chapter, couples must learn mindful communication in order to keep their relationship healthy and long-lasting. Mindful communication can help prevent conflicts because you and your partner will learn the art of reading and understanding each other's non-verbal cues; things that are left unsaid; and emotional reactions. You will also develop the art of active listening.

The following questions are inspired by the book, 201 Relationship Questions: The Couple's Guide to Building Trust and Emotional Intimacy [20]. Some of these questions may be awkward, or even scary, but they are designed to help you and your partner gain deeper insights about each other, feel comfortable and safe enough to allow yourselves to be vulnerable, to learn how to genuinely listen with your heart and mind, and nurture deeper intimacy in your relationship.

In most situations, asking questions demonstrates an interest in what the other person has to say - a desire to learn and understand. The following questions should not be cause for judgment or criticism. They should not be asked in such a way that will make your partner feel as if they are being tested and graded.

They should be asked because you honestly want to know what your partner has to say so that you can work together in resolving conflicts. They should be asked in such a way that will make your partner feel cherished, that they are significant.

These questions will not only help you better understand your partner - their fears, longings, frustrations, motivations, and pain; you might also help them dig deeper into themselves, become more self-aware, and grow fully into who they are and can be. At the end of this exercise, you and your partner should feel closer than ever, and your bond, stronger.

Questions For Deeper Insight

1. What specific things can I do to make you feel loved?
2. Are there actions or behaviors that I engage in which make you feel unloved or unappreciated?
3. Do you feel that our intimacy needs more work?

4. Do you feel that certain aspects of our relationship need to be revived or improved?

5. Are there things that you think are hurting our relationship and getting in the way of our closeness?

6. What can we do to revive our love and closeness?

7. Are there times when you feel I'm distant or disinterested?

8. Are there things that I say or do that make you feel disrespected?

9. What can I say or do to let you know that I respect you?

10. How would you like me to communicate a concern or issue I have about us, you, and other aspects of our life?

11. Do you feel that I don't genuinely listen to you when you have something to say?

12. What emotional needs do you feel I need to care more about?

13. Are there certain things that you don't want me to joke about, or certain things that you wish I would take more seriously?

14. Are you unhappy/unsatisfied with our sex life?

15. What are your thoughts on how we can make sex better for each other?

16. If one of us were to have a change of heart and mind about our spirituality or religious beliefs, how should we handle it?

17. What steps should we take when one or both of us lose our temper during an argument?

18. Do you feel that I'm getting in the way of your social life, or your relationship with your family?

19. Do you wish to spend more time alone, with your friends, your parents, or other family members?

20. What activities can we do to grow together as a couple?

21. Do you have childhood wounds that I can help heal, and how can I help?

22. What topics are you sensitive about and which trigger anger, pain, or resentment in you?

23. What do you need from me when you are feeling down, stressed, or worried?

24. What personal dreams and goals do you still wish to achieve in the near future?

25. Are there aspects of our shared life that you feel we should prioritize more?

Questions To Rekindle Romance

1. Do you remember the exact moment when you first realized you're in love with me?

2. What are your favorite memories of us?

3. Do you still remember our first kiss and how it made you feel? How can I make you feel that way again?

4. What is your idea of a romantic evening/date/getaway?

5. What do you consider romantic gestures?

6. What words make you feel loved, adored, and excited?

7. What is the perfect romantic gift?

8. What kind of surprises would you appreciate the most?

9. How do I make you feel like a woman/man? How do I make you better?

10. What do you appreciate and love most about me?

11. When do you find me at my most attractive? Least attractive?

12. What can I do to make you feel attractive and desired?

13. Do you think our romance needs work? How can we keep it alive until we're old and gray?

14. Are there aspects of our lives that you think might get in the way of romance? How can we fix this?

15. How do you like to be shown affection? How often?

16. What do I do/can I do to make you feel close to me?

17. How should I communicate my need for more romance?

18. How do you want me to respond to your needs?

19. How can we add more fun and excitement to our relationship?

20. What specific gestures from me remind you of how much I love you?

Questions To Explore Deeper Intimacy

1. What do I do/can I do to turn you on?

2. Do you like it when I initiate sex and in what ways?

3. What kind of foreplay gets you in the right mood?

4. Are there new things you want to try to make our foreplay more exciting?

5. Are there areas in our sex life that you think can be improved?

6. Do you have sexual fantasies that you'd like me to satisfy?

7. What new things or activities can we introduce into our sex life that you feel will make it more fun and satisfying? Do you want to try out certain sex toys?

8. What gestures/actions do you find highly erotic and arousing?

9. What outfits do you find me sexiest in?

10. What part of my body do you find sexiest?

11. Do you want to try out costumes or role-playing during sex?

12. How do you think can we keep the sexual energy between us alive when we're not together and in between our sexual encounters?

13. How often do you want to have sex? Do you prefer certain times of the day for sex?

14. Are there other places outside of our bedroom where you would enjoy making love?

15. What after-sex gestures do you like?

16. Do you like dirty/sexy talk before, during, and after sex?

17. What are your hard limits when it comes to sex and sexual explorations?

18. Do you feel that our sex life has gotten boring or become too much like a routine or a chore?

19. What aspects of our life do you think are getting in the way of a healthy sex life?

20. Do you think sex and improving our sex life can help get us closer? How?

21. Do you have insecurities about our sex life that I can address?

22. Are there things that I do during foreplay, sex, and after that you don't enjoy?

23. What should we do if one of us wants more sex than the other?

24. What does great sex mean to you? Can you describe it?

25. What is one of the best sexual encounters we've shared and why do you consider it as such?

Additional Questions For Better Understanding And Closeness

1. What's the worst date you've ever had?
2. What's the most embarrassing experience you've had that you don't usually share, if at all?
3. Do you have a childhood dream or desire that you still want to be fulfilled?
4. What five words best describe you?
5. What five words do you think best describe me? Us?
6. Are you most like your mom or dad? How?
7. If there was one thing about you that you could change, what would it be and why?
8. If you were given one chance to go back in time, at what age would you go back and why?
9. Who are the three people you most admire and look up to?
10. If money was not an issue, what's the first thing you'd spend it on?
11. What smell brings back a fond memory, and what memory is it?
12. What single, big change will make the world a better place?

13. If you could live anywhere in the world, where would it be?

14. Where and how do you picture us when we're 80?

15. What are the three biggest risks you'd take?

Sit With Each Other In Silence

You can do this before beginning a communication exercise or a simple heart-to-heart talk; in the middle, especially if you need to take a breather; or at the end, to assure each other that things are still alright.

Just take five minutes to sit in silence, with uninterrupted eye contact, perhaps also holding hands or with your knees touching. Soon, you'll notice that your breathing is in perfect rhythm with your partner's. Try to empty your mind of any thoughts, and just be present in that moment. Look deeply into each other's eyes without anger, resentment, or any other negative feelings. Or lean your foreheads against each other, close your eyes, and listen to each other's breaths; take pleasure in the other's presence.

Conclusion

Honest and respectful communication can prevent and solve most relationship problems. All healthy, happy, and lasting relationships have this in common. It won't be an exaggeration to say that good communication is just as important as love to make a relationship succeed.

Most relationships fail when communication fails. While there are lucky couples for whom good communication comes easily no matter the situation, most couples struggle to express themselves even simply during the course of their day-to-day lives and especially in times of conflict. Simple misunderstandings can quickly pile up and lead to unexpressed confusion, hurt, anger, and resentment. Sooner or later, the failure to properly communicate will lead to the worst possible means of communication - destructive arguments.

It is often said that if a relationship is right, then it will be easy; it should not take too much effort. This fairy-tale-kind of relationship is the exception, however. In the real world, the rule is that you have to put in a lot of work to make a relationship work. And a big part of this work must go towards cultivating and maintaining healthy communication. Just as importantly, both partners have to be equally committed to putting in the work.

Healthy communication is more than just about expressing ourselves through words. We say a lot without speaking - with our tone of voice, facial expressions, gestures, body posture, and even with what we refuse to say or do. The choices we make that affect our relationship also convey meaning. Some of the meanings we convey are intentional, others are not. In both cases, as long as our heart is in the right place, what we communicate will help strengthen our bond with our partner.

Despite our best intentions, however,

misunderstandings can still occur. This is mostly because we cannot control how the other person interprets and reacts to what we are trying to "say." During times when we are misunderstood, we should try to be more understanding; after all, we know exactly what we mean and it is our responsibility to clarify the misunderstanding.

Another key aspect of healthy communication is proper listening. As previously mentioned, communication is a two-way street. Knowing how to properly listen to both verbal and non-verbal messages will not only help avoid misunderstandings and conflict; it will also encourage our partner to communicate with us openly and honestly.

Good communication skills can be learned. The important thing is to work together and help each other. We should not be afraid to feel vulnerable; we should be comfortable with emotional and intellectual intimacy; we should be ready and willing to love in spite of the differences we have with our loved ones and regardless of their mistakes and shortcomings. Only when we are able to completely share ourselves with our partner and vice versa can there be good communication in our relationship.

References

1. Johnson, S. (2008) Hold Me Tight: Seven Conversations for a Lifetime of Love. Massachusetts: Little, Brown and Company.

2. Patterson, K. Grenny, J. McMillan, R. and Switzler, A. (2011) Crucial Conversations: Tools for Talking When Stakes Are High. 2nd edn. New York: McGraw-Hill Education.

3. Wile, D. (1993) After the Fight: Using Your Disagreements to Build a Stronger Relationship. New York: The Guilford Press.

4. Doell, F. (2003) Partners' listening styles and relationship satisfaction: listening to understand vs. listening to respond [online]. Available at: https://www.library.yorku.ca/find/Record/176 2898.

5. Lazare, A. (2005) On Apology. Oxford: Oxford University Press

6. Gottman, J. (2011) The Science of Trust: Emotional Attunement for Couples. 1st edn. New York: W. W. Norton & Company.

7. Shimberg. E.F. (1999) Blending Families. New York: Berkley Books.

8. Temple, M. (2009) The Marriage Turnaround: How Thinking Differently About Your Relationship Can Change Everything. Illinois: Moody Publishers.

9. Poulsen, S. (2008) A Fine Balance: The Magic Ratio to a Healthy Relationship [online]. Available at: https://www.extension.purdue.edu/extmedia/cfs/cfs-744-w.pdf.

10. Gottman, J. and Gottman, J. (2019) Eight Dates: Essential Conversations for a Lifetime of Love. New York: Workman Publishing Company.

11. Aron, A. Melinat, E. Aron, E. Vallone, R.D. and Bator, R. (1997) The Experimental Generation of Interpersonal Closeness: A Procedure and Some Preliminary Findings [online]. Available at: https://journals.sagepub.com/doi/pdf/10.1177/0 146167297234003.

12. Anwar, Y. (2015) Creating love in the lab: The 36 questions that spark intimacy [online]. Available at: https://news.berkeley.edu/2015/02/12/love-in-the-lab/.

13. Norman, C. and Aron, E.N. (2000) Couples' shared participation and novel and arousing activities and experienced relationship quality [online]. Available at: https://www.researchgate.net/profile/Elaine_Ar on/publication/12609069_Couples'_shared_part icipation_in_novel_and_arousing_activities_and _experienced_relationship_quality/links/5577bd 0f08aeacff20004ef3.pdf.

14. Gottman, J. and Gottman, J.S. (2019) Eight Dates: Essential Conversations for a Lifetime of Love. New York: Workman Publishing Company.

15. O'Leary, K.D. Acevedo, B. and Aron, A. (2011) Is Long-Term Love More Than A Rare Phenomenon? If So, What Are Its Correlates? [online]. Available at: https://journals.sagepub.com/doi/abs/10.1177/19 48550611417015?rss=1.

16. Greene, R. (2001) The Art of Seduction. 1st edn. New York: Viking Publishing.

17. Gottman, J. (2002) The Relationship Cure. New York: Random House.

18. Driver, J. and Gottman, J.M. (2004) Daily marital interactions and positive affect during marital conflict among newlywed couples [online]. Available   at:

https://www.ncbi.nlm.nih.gov/pubmed/1538695
6.

19. Barth, F.D. (2015) 6 Surprising Ways to Communicate Better With Your Partner [online]. Available at: https://www.psychologytoday.com/us/blog/the-couch/201501/6-surprising-ways-communicate-better-your-partner.

20. Davenport, B. (2015) 201 Relationship Questions: The Couple's Guide to Building Trust and Emotional Intimacy. California: CreateSpace Independent Publishing Platform.

Disclaimer

The information contained in **"THE ART OF MARRIAGE COMMUNICATION"** and its components, is meant to serve as a comprehensive collection of strategies that the author of this book has done research about. Summaries, strategies, tips and tricks are only recommendations by the author, and reading this book will not guarantee that one's results will exactly mirror the author's results.

The author of this book has made all reasonable efforts to provide current and accurate information for the readers of this book. The author and its associates will not be held liable for any unintentional errors or omissions that may be found.

The material in the book may include information by third parties. Third party materials comprise of opinions expressed by their owners. As such, the author of this book does not assume responsibility or liability for any third party material or opinions.

written expressed and signed permission from the author.

Manufactured by Amazon.ca
Bolton, ON